BEARS

A PORTRAIT OF THE ANIMAL WORLD

Robert Elman

TODTRI

This book was designed and produced by
Todtri Productions Limited
P.O. Box 572
New York, NY 10116-0572
Fax: (212) 695-6984

Printed and bound in China

ISBN 1-880908-16-6

Author: Leonard Lee Rue III

Publisher: Robert M. Tod
Book Designer: Mark Weinberg
Editor: Mary Forsell
Photo Editor: Natasha Milne
Design Associate: Jackie Skroczky
Typsetting: Command-O, NYC

INTRODUCTION

Bears have always fascinated, amused, and terrified man— and man often misinterprets their behaviour. These Alaskan brown bears may appear ready to fight (as sometimes they do, ferociously) but their sitting positions indicate nothing more serious than rough play.

Throughout history—indeed, beginning with our prehistoric ancestors—man has been mystified, fascinated, amused, and frequently terrified by bears. There is good reason for each of those reactions.

Bears exemplify the mysteries of the wilderness. At times they move with ghostly silence and hide so well that their presence goes undetected by human intruders in their domain. When angered (or occasionally when playful) they may crash through brush and snap small trees, and their echoing roars, coughs, grunts, and mouth-popping can sound supernatural as well as terrifying.

Their life cycle is fascinating in many ways. A newborn black bear cub, for example, is about the size of a squirrel without a tail, but at maturity it will have gained at least five hundred times its birth weight. A mother grizzly or polar bear may weigh 750 times as much as one of its newborn cubs—which probably weighs less than 1.5 pounds (.68 kilogram). To appreciate the disparity, contrast that with an average

This big male American black bear, advancing with its mouth open, may appear to be threatening but—at this point—is merely investigating. Its head would probably be lowered if it intended to charge. An old Native American saying advises that 'a bear with his head down is an unhappy bear'. Wisdom, however, demands keeping one's distance from any wild bear.

human mother who weighs only fifteen to twenty times as much as her infant.

All the same, a mother bear may occasionally look like a fat, hairy parody of the human mother, for a sow bear sometimes nurses a cub or two while lying on her back or sitting on her haunches with her back against a tree and the young on her lap. And at various times she is likely to behave toward her toddlers as lovingly— or as irritably—as a human mother. In a bear's antics, we see ourselves transformed, like victims of a witch's spell in a fairy tale, and the anthropomorphic impression amuses us. This, perhaps, is why we also find amusement in the performing bears at circuses, ponderously dancing, riding a tricycle, balancing on a slack rope or a ball, hugging and 'kissing' the trainer.

Lovable and amusing though bears may be, they are unpredictable and very dangerous— every living bear beyond the age of a year or so. There are renowned animal trainers who play roughly, confidently, fearlessly with enormous, exceedingly powerful bears they have raised lovingly from infancy. An adult bear of almost any species can crush a trainer's

skull with one bite or lacerate his flesh to the bone with one slap. A trainer's 'pet' bear, however well trained, essentially remains forever wild, and the trainer avoids danger only because he knows 'his' bear so well and is so expert in every aspect of handling the animal. A trained bear may be amusing, but to many it is also a terribly saddening sight, a creature out of its element, captive, made to perform demeaning tricks instead of living as it was born to live. To many, it is a victim of human witches more heartless than those in fairy tales, who have turned it into something less noble and magnificent than its true identity.

A large male polar bear leaps to an ice floe—not to avoid the water but simply because this is the quickest, easiest way to get there. A polar bear can swim 50 miles (80 kilometres) without resting.

BEARS IN LEGEND, LITERATURE, AND ART

Two cubs are the norm, but a healthy sow bear occasionally gives birth to three. These are American black bears in the western part of their range, where their colour is extremely variable. Note that the mother and one cub are cinnamon, the other two black.

Man has sought to understand and portray bears for many thousands of years. Some of Europe's cave paintings depict bearlike creatures, probably the ancestors of today's European brown bears but possibly an extinct species known as the cave bear. The ancients perceived mythical bears in the heavens and named the constellations containing the Big Dipper and Little Dipper Ursa Major (Great Bear) and Ursa Minor (Small Bear). Some Native American peoples referred to bears as their spiritual relatives, calling them Grandmother or Brother. There were transmutation legends—bear-people and people-

bears—and among the Dakota Indians a boy's puberty rites included remaining for days in a pit called a bear hole, fasting and imitating a bear.

The fairy tales of the Brothers Grimm, transcribed from recited folklore, included stories of ferocious bears, and European folklore also contains legends of bears that tricked people or were tricked by them. Probably the most famous of all such tales is 'Goldilocks and the Three Bears', a classic story still so popular among children that during the past decade at least eight hardcover editions were in print in the United States, including one accompanied by an audiocassette and one in sign language.

The prehistoric cave bears were the basis for centuries of dragon lore. Among the

After snuffling about in the snow, prospecting for small prey, a big northern bear stands erect to look around. People living in the American Northwest sometimes refer to a bear of this colour as a chocolate grizzly.

With ample fishing room for all, several bears gather on rock slabs and gravel bars in the McNeil River, Alaska. Gulls gather in force to pluck scattered morsels and discarded skins. Bears tolerate the birds until they become bothersome, then growl and lunge, temporarily scattering them.

sites where the fossilised bones of cave bears accumulated were Drachenloch in Switzerland and Drachenfels in Germany—the so-called Dragons' Caves. The skulls, substantially larger than those of present-day European bears and characterised by a steeply sloping forehead, gave rise to the dragon legends. It was at Drachenfels that Siegfried was supposed to have slain his dragon. In the mid nineteenth century, Richard Wagner, after studying Norse myths and the German Siegfried legend, wrote the poems and musical dramas that coalesced into *Der Ring des Nibelungen*. Thus did bears furnish—however indirectly—part of the inspiration for Wagnerian opera.

URSINE EVOLUTION AND MODERN SPECIES

From the somewhat incomplete fossil record, paleontologists believe that the ancestors of modern bears began to evolve early in the Oligocene epoch, some thirty to forty million years ago, as one of several groups of small animals branching from carnivorous tree climbers called miacids. From this same primeval stock are descend-

Every bear seems to develop its own fishing style, probably based on initial successes. Most face downstream or across-stream to intercept fish swimming upstream, but this Alaskan brown succeeds by 'tailing' them.

These grizzly cubs, trying to follow their mother's example, are using their eyes to search for some unfamiliar presence she has already seen. With muzzle raised, the mother is testing the air—using its nose, not its eyes.

Near Alaska's McNeil River, renowned as a magnet for salmon-hungry bears, a mother grizzly holds her cubs on her lap. They have just finished nursing and have clambered higher on her chest to play.

ed a second group, the raccoons and coatis, and a third comprising the canine species—wolves, foxes, coyotes, dogs.

All three modern groups—bears, raccoons, and canines—are exceptionally intelligent by comparison with most other mammals, yet the ancestral miacids had small brains relative to their body size and could not have been blessed with comparable intelligence. A possible explanation of this paradox is the theory that primeval prey was easy to capture, but during the ensuing millions of years some of the prey species became more wary and elusive. As the prey became smarter, natural selection favored more efficient predators, and the bears, raccoons, and canines survived by evolving larger, better-developed brains.

Some paleontologists hold that the oldest known creature that legitimately could be called a bear was *Ursavus elemensis*, a dog-sized predator inhabiting subtropical

The polar bear's diet of ringed seals (the Arctic's most abundant large mammal), bearded seals, and an occasional disabled walrus ends wherever a summer thaw drives bears ashore. Here, a mother bear, two cubs, and a subadult search for eggs, nestlings, rodents, and berries. Good fortune may also bring them a caribou calf.

These cubs are just over a year old. When playing in trees, one will often clamber onto a higher branch and swat at the sibling below, but rarely if ever is a cub dislodged.

11

All bears love water—if it provides a food resource. These are Asian brown bears of the Manchurian subspecies in the act of disputing fishing rights. They may be siblings, and their sparring will be brief and bloodless.

Two young brown bears practice their budding fishing skills in a northern river.

This is a lactating Kodiak grizzly whose cubs are unquestionably waiting for her on the bank of the stream—and she is evidently peering at them, confirming their safety. With its fur wetly plastered to its body, the mother bear's four pectoral nipples are visible. It also has a pair of inguinal nipples, believed by most researchers to be used chiefly or only during den life.

Striking colour variations occur even within a single subspecies of brown bear occupying a relatively small geographic range. These two resting bruins are Alaskan brown bears showing the pale tone known as blond.

Although polar bears are more uniform in hue than other ursine species, they do not always look white. When the sun is low in the Arctic, they can appear golden, and in summer and autumn their fur is often 'rusted' by the oxidising effect of the sun.

Europe some twenty million years ago. Larger, more bearlike bears existed about six million years ago, and soon (that is, soon in geological terms) evolved into many forms, a few of them gigantic. However, many of those species met with extinction, probably doomed by changing climate and habitat. Our modern bears are thought to be descended from a relatively small animal, *Protursus*, which, before it became extinct, finally gave rise to the modern genus *Ursus* two to three million years ago. Its descendants splintered into three lineages, one in Europe that was the antecedent of the extinct cave bear, *U. spelaus*, and two in Asia that brought forth today's brown bears on three

The brown bear at left may be standing in chest-deep water, but the one at right is probably sitting. If this were a serious battle, each would rise up, standing as high as possible while biting and slapping at its adversary.

continents and the black bear in America.

At least two other bear species, both very large, once roamed wide portions of North America. The Florida cave bear ranged from the Gulf Coast up into what is now Tennessee, and the short-faced bear was distributed from Alaska to Mexico and eastward across the continent to Virginia.

The latter was probably the largest of all the Ice Age bears, more than 5 feet (1.52 metres) high at the shoulder when walking normally—not rising up on its hind legs—and at least fifteen percent larger than today's Alaskan coastal grizzlies (a very big subspecies of brown bear). Grizzlies have been known to kill full-grown moose, and everything about the fossils of the short-faced bear indicates that it could easily kill the largest prehistoric mammals.

Most of the present forms of bears have probably been in existence for less than a million years. America's black bears evidently came from Asian ancestors and were well established long before grizzlies arrived in America. The earliest brown bears are thought to have occurred in

China. They spread through Asia and Europe and finally, during the Ice Age, crossed the Bering Strait land bridge to North America. Youngest of the modern species is the polar bear, which evidently evolved from coastal Siberian brown bears—according to some estimates only a hundred thousand years ago, and according to other estimates a little more than a quarter of a million years ago. Eventually, its

A black bear walking through the woods will generally flee at the approach of a human, but if startled, has been known to kill.

This is an Asian brown bear, photographed in China. Scientists believe that all of today's brown bears—more than fifty subspecies occurring in Asia, Europe, and North America—evolved in China.

A spectacled bear, photographed in the Andes Mountains of Venezuela, exhibits the shaggy coat characteristic of the species. The facial markings on this specimen form broken eyebrows and a bib rather than spectacles.

A polar bear rises on its hind legs to savour a wind-carried scent of prey—most likely a seal. Eskimo and Indian legends described bears as the beasts that stand like a man, and sometimes referred to them as spiritual relatives, calling them such names as Grandmother or Brother.

A polar bear gnaws packed snow from its paws. This may be how some polar bears have learned to hold one paw in a similar position, camouflaging the black nose, while stalking a seal.

Sometimes a rest stop can also serve as a cooling stop. On snow-strewn ice, a yearling polar bear sprawls flat, pressing as much of its body as possible against the frigid surface.

A brown bear grazes in a meadow edging an Alaskan stream. Grass is among the earliest vegetation to become lush after bears emerge from their dens, and provides nutrition in a moist, easily digestible form that seems to help the animals start their alimentary systems functioning normally again.

Bears have better vision than most observers realise, but are thought to be fully or partially colour-blind. It is undoubtedly scent that often attracts them to flowering plants, which in many cases provide excellent nutrition.

This American
black bear can
surely find a
stream or pond
close by, but there
is more enjoyment
in licking dew or
clinging raindrops
from a young
conifer—along
with any insects
hidden among
the needles.

This black bear
in Yellowstone
National Park—
a typical represen-
tative of the brown
Western colour
phase—is guarding
the carcass of a
mule deer. If the
deer was very old,
very young, injured,
or sick, the bear
may have killed it.
More likely it was
a lucky find, dead
when the bear
located it by scent.

numbers spread around the globe in arctic and subarctic latitudes where vegetation is sparse or absent. Adapting to such harsh habitat, it not only acquired its white coat but also developed extremely specialised feeding habits, becoming the most truly carnivorous of the bear family. In many parts of its circumpolar range, a polar bear can live on seals alone.

A very different animal that is strikingly bearlike in appearance is the panda, sometimes called panda bear. Some taxonomists now regard it as belonging to a distinct genus of the true bear family, but its correct taxonomic classification remains in dispute. It, too, is descended from the miacids.

An Alaskan grizzly bear grazes as contentedly—and gluttonously—as a buffalo in lush grasslands. Bears consume large quantities of grass in spring and summer. Another kind of springtime feast is provided by skunk cabbage on stream banks and tidal flats.

This undeniably grey bear may look positively blue when the light is dim or hazy. Known as the blue bear or glacier bear, it was long regarded as a distinct species, but is actually a subspecies of American black bear found only at Yakutat Bay, Alaska, a mountainous coastal strip less than 100 miles (160 kilometres) long.

When on the hunt, an Alaskan brown bear is alert to every movement, sight, and scent.

Scientists long regarded it as more closely allied to raccoons than to bears but not very closely related to either. Recent morphological and genetic studies indicate that the panda is more closely related to bears, but it will be hardly surprising if the scientists eventually agree that it belongs in its own unique classification, distinct from both raccoons and true bears. A unique creature with a modified wrist bone in the forepaws that forms a sixth digit and functions like a thumb, it is about as dexterous as a raccoon but more herbivorous than either bears or raccoons. Unfortunately, one thing it has in common with most bears is its severely endangered status.

Even within the genera of the true bears, scientists do not always agree completely about the divisions of species and, especially, subspecies. It is possible, however, to list the various species on which there is general agreement:

Not every white bear is a polar bear. This handsome animal is a Kermode bear—a little-known British Columbian subspecies of the black bear—and it would be almost snow-white if its fur were not stained by earth, the juices of vegetation, and minerals oxidised by the sun.

Even a glacier bear as large as this one will spend many hours chewing grass or digging and lapping up insects. A single blade or a single ant would have almost no nutritional value, but a bear gleans them by the thousands.

- **American Black Bear** (*Ursus americanus*)
- **Asian Black, or Moon, Bear** (*Selenarctos thibetanus*)
- **Brown Bear, including Alaskan Brown Bear and Grizzly Bear** (*U. arctos*)
- **Polar Bear** (*U. maritimus*)
- **Sloth, or Indian, Bear** (*Melursus ursinus*)
- **Spectacled, or Andean, Bear** (*Tremarctos ornatus*)
- **Sun, or Malayan, Bear** (*Helarctos malayanus*)

SIZING UP A BRUIN

A 350-pound (157-kilogram) black bear may seem surprisingly small when viewed from a distance; indeed, so may a grizzly bear weighing twice as much. Upon first seeing bears in the wild, people are often surprised by animals that appear smaller than expected. This is merely because bears are round-bodied, low-slung creatures whose legs are short by comparison with torso size, and the thickness of the legs adds to the illusion of squatness.

That same 350-pound bear is considerably taller than an average man when it rises up on its hind legs to sniff for food or alien scent, listen for any intrusive sounds, and scan its surroundings for the sight of anything that needs to be avoided, attacked, or eaten. (Bears have the reputa-

Polar bears are such skillful underwater swimmers that they occasionally catch unwary fish. Sometimes they also swim underwater to sneak up on a seal that basks on the edge of an ice floe. They lunge up out of the water with incredible speed and force to snatch the prey.

tion of being nearsighted, chiefly because they seem to ignore stationary objects or creatures unless fairly close, relying on scent and sound more than on vision. But anyone in bear country will do well to remember that experiments have proved bears to have fairly keen eyes—and nothing escapes their hearing and olfactory senses.) As for the grizzly, which attains twice the weight of the black bear, when it rises on its hind legs it may tower 9 feet (2.73 metres) tall, and a mature male Alaskan brown bear is often considerably larger.

The various species of bears encompass a surprisingly wide range of body weights and sizes. At maturity, the sun bear of the southeast Asian tropics quite often weighs no more than 80 pounds (36 kilograms)— great size being of no particular advantage in a hot climate. With obvious exceptions such as the elephant, animals near the equator tend to be smaller than those in the north—especially those belonging to the same family. This is because a large animal conserves heat more efficiently than a small one. Alaskan brown bears (or coastal grizzlies, as they are also known) generally

A half-grown brown bear runs through the shallows, chasing fish. The young learn the rudiments by watching their elders, but are generally overeager to try what they see. At first they tend to be very clumsy at catching fish, timing their grabs and lunges poorly.

attain a weight between 800 and 1,200 pounds (360 to 540 kilograms) at eight or nine years of age, and one Kodiak brown bear was reported to weigh 1,656 pounds (745 kilograms).

Male polar bears vie with Alaskan browns for the rank of world's largest carnivorous mammals. At maturity, females generally weigh well over 700 pounds (315 kilograms), and males generally weigh about 1,000 (450 kilograms). The largest specimen ever recorded weighed 2,210 pounds (994 kilograms)—over a ton!

Although a polar bear will eat whatever meat it finds, including anything from gulls to whale carcasses or other such carrion, seals are its chief prey and it hunts them with uncanny efficiency. Brown bears are far more omnivorous, but the main reason the Alaskan browns attain such gigantic proportions is the easy availability of protein in the form of salmon— seemingly countless salmon struggling their way up Alaska's shallow streams during the spawning runs. A brown bear will also dig out hibernating marmots, excavating huge pits in the tundra with claws and feet powerful enough to demolish per-

mafrost, and it will feast on carrion or any live prey it manages to catch. All the same, even the largest Alaskan brown bear generally devours considerably more vegetation than meat in the course of a year.

Thus these strange animals can be accurately described not only as the world's largest mammalian carnivores but also as the least carnivorous of carnivores.

A Malayan sun bear lies supine—just as European and American bears often do—while nursing her cub. A mother bear usually exhibits strong affection for the cubs until she accepts a new mate, at which time the male evicts them.

Though very inquisitive, cubs stay close to their mothers, and brown bear cubs stay especially close. The one at the rear, hugging the mother, is not seeking affection but protection from the photographer.

So young that its nose is still very pink, this cub has already learned how to climb a tree quickly and hide there. Tree climbing provides exercise, access to edible vegetation and insects, and escape from enemies such as adult male bears, which will attack cubs. The fur of this American black bear will remain brown, but its nose will turn black.

HUMAN CONFLICT AND CONSERVATION

Seen in low Arctic light, a polar bear may actually appear as a black silhouette as it searches for prey. So uncanny is its scenting ability that field researchers have reported polar bears that detected prey over 20 miles (32 kilometres) away and marched straight to it. They can easily detect seal dens hidden under 3 feet (.91 metre) of snow and ice.

No matter how vehemently people proclaim their love of wild creatures—and particularly creatures as beguiling as bears—man in general has always had an ambivalent attitude, a love-hate relationship with bears. Man is capable of truly loving the creatures he hunts, and he has hunted bears since the epoch when both dwelt in caves. For just as long, bears have occasionally hunted men, though not often for food—more commonly to defend cubs or a food source from an alien intruder, or to eliminate an intruder perceived as either a potential threat or a potential competitor for available food sources, or sometimes

out of mere curiosity or irritability. And although a bear may kill a human for reasons other than hunger, once it has done so it is quite likely to feast on that human after or even before the victim is dead. There is good reason to be respectful if not afraid of bears in the wild and to give them a wide berth.

Even the American black bear, which usually flees at the approach of a human, has been known to kill. Some other species, including the polar bear, are feared for their sudden, seemingly unprovoked surges of ferocity. The American subspecies of brown bear known as the grizzly, whose full scientific designation is, quite aptly, *Ursus arctos horribilis*, is notorious for its murderous attacks, but no more so than

A growling Alaskan brown bear, or coastal grizzly, bares its teeth in a threat display. It does not necessarily mean an attack is imminent, but it should be warning enough to any intruder.

U. a. middendorffi, the Alaskan brown bear, with which it sometimes interbreeds.

The Asian black bear, or moon bear, is justly feared throughout its range. This animal is short tempered not only when guarding cubs or a food source but also when inadvertently disturbed in a winter den. It does not hibernate as deeply as the American black bear, and when awakened tends to be both alert and enraged. One thing it does have in common with the American black bear is its habit of eating tree leaves, buds, fruits, and nuts, and stripping the bark from certain trees to eat the cambium. In Japan the most valuable timber species, cedar and cypress, seem to suffer most. In the course of raiding Japanese agricultural lands, this species also occasionally kills people. Little wonder that the Japanese, in turn, annually kill as many as three thousand bears, both as nuisances or menaces and for sport.

The moon bear is hardly unique in appropriating what man intends to harvest for himself. The sloth bear of India and Sri Lanka loves to feed on sugarcane, corn, yams, and the mohwa flowers that Indian villagers ferment to make a beverage. The villagers retaliate, of course. South America's spectacled, or Andean, bear is another raider of corn and sugarcane, and an occasional killer of livestock like the grizzly and Alaskan brown bears. Even the American black bear, though less predaceous than the grizzly, has been known to kill livestock, and in America's Northwest—particularly in the state of Washington—has sometimes reduced the profits of the timber industry by girdling trees for their cambium.

The world's southernmost population of polar bears, ranging along the lower western edge of Hudson Bay in Manitoba, moves inland during summer and then gathers every autumn around the little town of Churchill (Canada's northernmost deepwater port but better known as Polar Bear Capital of the World). There the animals await the formation of sufficient ice to permit their migration up the bay, where they resume their seal hunting. Though polar bears are more strictly carnivorous than any other bear species, while on land they must eat what they can find, including vegetation, misguided handouts from foolhardy humans, and the more or less edible refuse deposited at rubbish dumps. For that matter, bears the world over will raid rubbish dumps and campsites if any food is where they can reach it—or merely smell it.

Conflicts have been inevitable, although at Churchill they have been drastically reduced by various precautionary measures, warning signs for the benefit of tourists, and even the tranquilising and removal of habitual nuisance bears or noticeably dangerous ones. Conflicts with other species, inhabiting regions more heavily populated by humans, have been

Bears often bed down, particularly around midday. Often they scrape together a mat of leaves, twigs, and assorted debris in a tangled thicket to assure concealment and undisturbed rest, but occasionally they merely flop down and doze. This American black bear has been napping in a cedar swamp in early autumn.

An American black bear awakens from a nap and stretches. The humanlike motions and postures of bears have always inspired anthropomorphic interpretations. A cub kept as a pet by Theodore Roosevelt inspired the creation of the Teddy bear. This big male's chest chevron (more often a small, irregular blaze) is a common marking on black bears in the eastern United States.

far more frequent and disastrous. Such conflicts—including livestock losses—led to the extermination of grizzlies throughout most of the United States.

At the current time, a far worse problem is the illicit trade in furs and bear parts—specifically, the gallbladders, which are used in traditional Oriental medicines; and bear paws, the essential ingredient of one of the Orient's most coveted if costly soups. The profits of this trade are so tempting that a thriving international black market persists despite efforts to suppress it. With the exception of the American black bear, which is faring well and, in some parts of the United States and Canada, actually increasing in numbers, all of the world's bears are listed as endangered species in parts or all of their respec-

tive ranges. This is not to say that all are in danger of extinction. The grizzly is endangered or threatened below the Canadian border, with a population probably numbering fewer than eight hundred, almost all of them in and around Yellowstone Park. In Alaska and Canada, however, North America's brown bears, including the grizzlies, number about fifty thousand and their populations are both healthy and stable.

In some parts of Europe, brown bears are sufficiently abundant and reproducing in such numbers that several nations have permitted stringently regulated hunting. Various European governments are conducting habitat and wildlife management programmes aimed at increasing their bear populations. In fact, a programme has been

Yearling cubs like these American black bears may playfully threaten each other even while balancing on a tree branch, but they are unlikely to wrestle because they fear falling. They descend by clawing and scrambling down a trunk, rear end first.

Polar bears sometimes fight over food, but these two well-fed subadults are playing. They may be siblings or just 'friends'. When comfortably fat, two (or occasionally more) young polar bears often travel, hunt, and play together without hostility. Researchers have not yet discovered how long these attachments last.

trophy hunters. The polar bear populations are no longer dwindling in Canada, nor are they elsewhere.

The various Asian species are the bears most severely endangered. Trafficking in bear parts is prohibited by most nations and by international agreement, and the battle to stem it has reached nearly the proportions of the battle against smugglers of addictive drugs.

The International Union for the Conservation of Nature (IUCN) works closely with the World Wildlife Fund and other conservation organisations to con trol the illicit bear trade and to establish programmes aimed at increasing ursine populations. The International Association for Bear Research and Management, a professional organisation of research biologists and wildlife-management specialists, also works closely with the IUCN for the increase and stabilisation of these populations. Fortunately, progress is being made, but the future of bears remains clouded in many parts of the world.

There is no mistaking the tracks of a large brown bear. Bears are plantigrade animals that touch down with the entire soles of their feet, and the hind foot leaves an impression like that of a wide-footed human giant. The hind print of a really big Alaskan brown may be 10 inches (25 centimetres) wide at the front and nearly 17 inches (43 centimetres) long.

Fully mature brown bears lose their tree-climbing ability. Their claw structure is not well adapted to clasping or to pulling and pushing that much weight. Young brown bears do it quite well, however. This one is going after the eggs or nestlings of a bald eagle. The nest may be demolished in the ensuing battle if the bear reaches it.

undertaken to re-introduce bears into the French Alps. European brown bears occasionally prey on domestic sheep and cattle, but several countries now pay compensation to livestock owners instead of reducing the bear populations.

The fact remains, however, that in parts of its historic range the brown bear is endangered, as are the sun bear, the moon bear, the spectacled bear, the Indian bear, and even the polar bear. The word 'even' relates to the fact that all the nations having arctic or subarctic jurisdiction are now active in managing their polar bear populations, prohibiting hunting or other exploitation except in Canada, where Inuit subsistence hunters are allowed to take a small annual quota or use a very small percentage of that quota by guiding fee-paying

Sunrise near Churchill, Manitoba, bathes a polar bear in soft, rosy light. The bear's appearance of alert concentration probably indicates that the animal is watching for potential prey or keeping an eye on cubs.

Forestalling Tragic Encounters

Every year, people are killed by bears. Rarely will a bear follow and stalk a human being, although an animal with defective teeth or a disabled foot may be prospecting hungrily. More often, the bear detects an unfamiliar creature, approaches out of curiosity, and quickly perceives that the intruder is easy prey.

Attacks by mother bears guarding cubs are most common, but seldom happen in this manner. What does happen is that the bear detects an intruder belatedly—when the person is so near that the bear attacks instead of herding her cubs away.

To move through bear habitat quietly is a dangerous mistake. A safer procedure is to announce one's presence repeatedly, thus encouraging any nearby bear to retreat or detour. A hiker in bear country is wise to whistle, sing, occasionally shout, or talk to himself or a companion. Any companions should stay close to one another.

Tragic incidents are more frequent at campsites, because bears can smell food from great distances. A bear usually will go straight to the source of the aroma and demolish anything in the way. To make the situation still more dangerous, the animal may investigate or simply rip apart anything else nearby in frustration or on the chance of finding more food. This,

most often, is when a camper is assaulted in a sleeping bag or tent, or caught while trying to climb a tree.

The best safeguard is to store all food in sturdy, airtight containers, with no smears or crumbs on the outside, at a considerable distance from camp. If the store is hung from a high tree, any escaping scent will probably dissipate unnoticed, high over a bear's head. And although most bear species can climb trees, a container can be hung out of the animal's reach. A defeated bear may go on its way, but a successful one is likely to search for further bounty.

The tracks of a polar bear are very distinctive. The footprints are rounder than those of brown bears, somewhat blurred because the soles of the feet are furred, and form two close parallel lines. These bears wander immense distances.

39

Perhaps this American black bear will nudge her cub into the water, or the cub will wade the shallows of its own accord. If the mother perceives any danger, it will send the cub scurrying back into the woods.

This adult cinnamon black bear in California's Sierra Mountains looks too portly to climb a tree, but its paw-and-claw structure and very powerful legs can do it—though not as nimbly as a yearling can scamper up.

Grizzly cubs in Denali National Park explore the early summer vegetation.

This Alaskan bear has probably pounced, trying to pin a fish to the stream bottom. Bears have been seen to lose their balance and tumble or flounder in the water, but they immediately resume fishing, not at all disconcerted.

BEARS ON FOUR CONTINENTS

An excellent fishing station is at the top of a fall, where a brown bear can catch salmon as they leap and flop in a struggle to get over the barrier. Bears often catch fish in their mouths, but their styles are individual. Some swipe with a paw or try to pin a fish, and they may eat the prey there or carry it to a bar or bank.

The popular but erroneous perception of the world's bears includes perhaps three or four species, all inhabiting regions from the Arctic down to relatively cold forests in North America, Europe, and Russian Siberia. It is true that polar bears roam the ice floes and coasts of the Arctic Ocean and the North Atlantic, and that the brown bear in all its forms—probably some fifty subspecies, including the grizzly and Alaska's so-called Kodiak bear—primarily inhabits the northern halves of North America, Europe, and Asia. But the total global range of the bruin family extends into the Southern Hemisphere and the tropics.

The Brown Bear

Japan has a remnant population of brown bears (about three thousand) on the island of Hokkaido, at the same latitude as Manchuria's brown bears. On the Asian continent it ranges farther south, into southern China, India, and Iran. At one time it was fairly abundant in northern Mexico. Its way of life depends on remote mountain strongholds, not on northern latitudes, and it has a wider distribution than any other bear.

A boulder jutting above the surface of this stream in Katmai National Park, Alaska, gives a bear a fine view of passing fish but is too small for manoeuvring on all fours. The bear may very well dive in to make a catch.

Some bears totally submerge their heads to catch salmon swimming by. This brown bear in Alaska's Katmai National Park has just come up for air.

Two male brown bears dispute fishing rights. When they battle, they do so fiercely, but fatalities are rare, and an order of dominance is quickly established on the basis of size and aggressive display. Large males get the best fishing spots, and large females with cubs rank next.

This chocolate grizzly and blond grizzly are probably strangers to each other but could be siblings. They are testing each other for dominance, and one will soon back off. In Alaska, intergraded zones occupied by both coastal grizzlies (Alaskan brown bears) and inland grizzlies produce a wide range of sizes and fur tones.

American Black and Spectacled Bears

The American black bear ranges from Alaska eastward across the continent and southward to Florida, the Gulf Coast, and northern Mexico. The far less familiar spectacled bear (so named for its white or tawny facial markings, which are quite variable and do not always ring the eyes) exists in scattered populations from Venezuela southward through the Andes into Peru and northernmost Chile. South America's only bear, it is also called the Andean bear, another less than totally accurate name. It chiefly inhabits thickly forested mountain slopes but is also found on arid coastal scrublands.

The Sun Bear

The world's smallest species—not much bigger than a large dog and seldom exceeding 110 pounds (49.5 kilograms)—is the little black sun bear found in tropical and subtropical regions of southern and southeastern Asia, including the Malay Peninsula and the islands of Borneo, Sumatra, and Java. (The smallest bears are the tropical

For this black bear in Alaska's Tongass National Forest, the easiest way to handle a writhing catch is to back out of the stream with it. The bear will then use one or both paws to pin it down.

In Tongass National Forest, a black bear exhibits curiosity for the camera—evidence of the bear's naturally inquisitive nature.

South America's only ursine species, the spectacled bear is named for its facial markings, which sometimes circle the eyes but are extremely variable. Another, somewhat more accurate name for it is Andean bear, although it inhabits low coastal scrublands as well as the forested mountain range.

denizens and the largest are the northern brown and polar bears, for large bodies conserve heat more efficiently than small ones.) The sun bear is named for its pale or yellowish chest crescent; in Eastern folklore a yellow crescent represents the rising sun, though to Western eyes it resembles a crescent moon. This is another quite variable marking, sometimes absent, blackly speckled, or forming an irregular patch or bull's-eye.

The Asian Black Bear

The primary range of the Asian black bear extends farther north, into the Tibetan Himalayas, but it is also found in Japan, Taiwan, and as far south as Bangladesh and Laos. Additional common names for this species are Tibetan or Himalayan black bear and moon bear. The latter name refers to a white or ivory chest marking, usually a crescent or chevron but occasionally faint or absent. With equal accuracy it might also be called the ruffed bear, for the long black fur on the neck and shoulders forms a thick ruff, almost like a sideward-flaring mane.

Both sun bears and sloth bears have exceedingly long tongues, an excellent adaptation for reaching into deep recesses to extract the termites and other insects inhabiting tropical and subtropical habitat. This animal is a sun bear foraging in a dead tree.

The Asian black bear (this particular one a denizen of the Himalayas) is characterised by wide-set ears, a wide ruff of fur on neck and shoulders, and a dangerously irritable disposition when disturbed in its den. Ferocious in the wild but easily trained if captive from the time of cubhood, this species has been widely used in circuses (as have Indian bears and European browns). It is also called the moon bear in reference to a crescent marking on its chest.

A miniature among bruins, the sun bear is the world's smallest ursine species. This typical specimen may weigh less than 90 pounds (40 kilograms). Its very long, sharp, sickle-shaped claws aid it in climbing trees, breaking branches to make temporary arboreal beds, and tearing out insect nests to reach grubs and honey.

In Asian folklore, a yellow crescent symbolises the rising sun, and the sun bear's name is derived from the marking often seen on its neck and upper chest.

A mother sloth bear allows her large cub to clamber over her, playfully nipping and clawing. The cub's open mouth reveals that these bears lack front teeth between their canines; their unusual mouths, somewhat tubular and with a hollowed-out palate, are an adaptation for sucking termites and other insects out of their earthen tunnels.

This European brown bear belongs to the same species as the grizzly and Alaskan brown bears. Its genuinely intelligent and seemingly amused expression is often seen, and helps explain why bears figure prominently in myths and fairy tales. The gigantic skulls and bones of its ancestors gave rise to Europe's dragon legends.

Like all of its kin the world over, the sloth, or Indian, bear is quite comfortable sitting up on its haunches. This one has reached overhead to nibble a sprig of vegetation. Termites and honey top the list of its favourite foods.

The Indian Bear

In the late eighteenth century, a curator at the British Museum, misguided by fanciful descriptions and the long, deeply curved claws on strange skins sent from India by colonial big-game hunters, classified a new species as a 'bear sloth'—a sloth with bearish characteristics. But even a layman could see that it was a bear—albeit a very unusual, unbearish bear—and in 1810 the great French anatomist Georges Cuvier corrected the error by renaming it sloth bear. So it has been called ever since, although it is also, and more appropriately, called the Indian bear. This is a very adaptable species, found from the base of the Himalayas southward to the tip of India and the island of Sri Lanka, as far eastward as Assam, and in Nepal's Chitwan National Park. Deforestation has severely reduced its numbers, but it can live in a wide

In warm weather—warm for a polar bear—one of these creatures may come out of the water and go right back in just to play or cool itself. This one was photographed in the icy summer waters of Wager Bay, in the Northwest Territories of Canada.

variety of wooded habitat, from northern thorn forests to humid, tropical jungle.

This strange animal has a long, shaggy, rumpled coat of black, occasionally with glints of russet, and a wide, ragged ruff over the shoulders and neck. Usually the chest is marked by a white or rusty white chevron or U-shaped patch. The sparsely haired muzzle, whitish or grey, is longer than that of other bears and tends to be somewhat cylindrical—a useful adaptation for an animal that loves to suck termites out of their galleried hills.

The Polar Bear

The polar bear has unparalleled resistance to cold, resulting from several anatomical marvels. Sometimes the fur is stained, and in summer may turn yellowish from oxidation caused by the sun, but normally the coat appears to be ivory or snow-white because it reflects and scatters all visible rays of the spectrum. Actually, the individual outer hairs—guard hairs—are not white but clear and hollow. Many mammals have hollow guard hairs, an effective form of insulation, but a polar bear's are different.

Teaching her sizable but still dependent cubs to hunt seals, a mother polar bear herds them across the ice. By August they weigh over 100 pounds (45 kilograms) but will den with her longer than the young of other bear species—often for two more winters.

Its coat releases almost no heat—not even enough for the animals to be censused by aerial infra-red photography. Ultraviolet photography works, however, because snow reflects ultraviolet radiation while the fur absorbs it, creating a contrast. The clear, hollow hairs trap ultraviolet radiation and conduct it to the bear's skin—which is as black as the animal's nose and lips, and absorbs the heat. This radiation is caught from any direction and, for reasons not yet understood, the ultraviolet energy flows only inward to the skin, with almost none escaping. Astonishingly, this system is ninety-five percent efficient in converting the rays into usable heat.

The polar bear is the most strictly carnivorous of all ursine species, yet a large population inhabiting Hudson Bay moves inland during the warm months and subsists largely on vegetation until the spread of ice enables them to move out on the bay and resume seal hunting. This one is merely yawning, not warning competitors away.

But the air temperature may be well below zero, and a polar bear can still swim 50 miles (80 kilometres) through arctic water without resting—and without much exposure to the sun—so the heat conveyor alone would not suffice, nor would the woolly undercoat. Beneath the skin is a layer of fat, comparable to the blubber of marine mammals, which may be over 4 inches (10 centimetres) thick when winter arrives. It provides both insulation and buoyancy for swimming. Finally, the circulatory system incorporates a 'countercurrent' like a seal's to cool the blood as it flows toward the body's surface and warm it on the return flow—'an automatic heat engine', as one researcher described it.

Rest is wherever a polar bear finds it, and whenever the animal feels sleepy. This is a subadult on Hudson Bay, sleeping through a snow storm. Only a severe blizzard will prompt a polar bear to dig a shallow den in a snow bank.

After emerging from water, a polar bear frequently shakes its head and shoulders like a huge dog, sending spray in all directions.

BEAR BEHAVIOUR

Half asleep, an American black bear rests while her cubs comb her fur for wood ticks. At maturity, both cubs will have greyish or brown snouts, but the one at right may have a very dark brown coat rather than the black of its mother and sibling.

Young siblings, after their eventual eviction by a mother intent on mating again, sometimes forage and den together for another year, then go their separate ways. American black bears and grizzlies are fairly typical in reaching sexual maturity at three to five years of age, but the birth rate is low because a female must devote more than a full year to her young and therefore mates every two years. Two is the usual number of offspring, occasionally three, very rarely four.

As the urge to mate intensifies with the warming and lengthening of the days, a male begins to wander farther than usual from its normal foraging area. When he finds a receptive female, the pair will feed and travel together amicably, even demonstrating great affection for about a month. And then they part.

Pregnancy and Birth

If the period of pregnancy were comparable to that of most mammals, mating would have to occur in the autumn (when bears are preoccupied with fattening themselves before denning) to achieve birth in the spring—or else, with concep-

These Alaskan brown bears are copulating. At other times of year they would be hostile toward each other, but now, in spring or early summer, they may travel and feed together for as long as a month.

Tracked to its winter den, this American black bear is obviously torpid after being roused from hibernation. Asian black bears seem to awaken quickly if disturbed—even in mid-winter—but American bears are slower to regain their senses.

Early spring has arrived and the snow is melting, but this American black bear remains denned with her three cubs snuggled against—almost under—her. Drowsily, she will venture out before the cubs do, but in their eagerness to stay close they will soon follow.

These grizzly cubs, still mostly pink and grey, may already have doubled their birth weight, but at ten days of age neither their eyes nor their ears have yet opened.

tion in the spring, birth might occur before denning time and the young probably could not survive the winter. It seems likely that the remote ancestors of modern bears had a relatively short gestation period, but natural selection favored an evolutionary lengthening of pregnancy to achieve exquisite synchronisation with the denning habit that developed during cold glacial epochs. For most bear species, about six months elapses from conception to birth.

What happens is called delayed implantation. The fertilised eggs become tiny embryos and undergo the initial divisions common to mammals—but then cease development and do not become attached to the uterine wall. Instead, each embryo floats free in the uterus in a kind of suspended animation until autumn. Only then does it become implanted in the uterine wall. In bears of the far north, development resumes in September, a month or two before denning; in American black bears, it may resume as late as November, with denning to commence in December. Among species that den late in the year, subsequent embryon-

ic development is very swift, for birth takes place in January or February.

When it does take place, the mother is either unaware or barely aware of it—an enviable advantage over the human life cycle. Until quite recently, biologists were more or less in agreement that even northern bears are not true hibernators. That is, they don't become nearly as comatose as hibernating mammals

This three-month-old polar bear cub is totally dependent on its mother and is hurriedly waddling back to her after wandering a short distance away.

In the parts of America where both grizzlies and black bears dwell, colour is no indicator of species. Identification of this grizzly is easy, however, because of its conspicuous hump of shoulder muscle (probably evolved for digging out marmots and demolishing insect-ridden logs) and its slightly concave snout. A black bear would have a rounded shoulder and straight or slightly convex snout.

A sow grizzly and her young chase an arctic ground squirrel. This particular ground squirrel is far enough ahead so it will probably escape, but such hunting lessons are vital in the development of cubs.

A full-grown American black bear might be able to squeeze into this cavity, but the tree hollow is probably too high off the ground to serve as a den entrance. The cub merely likes to back into it and peer out, perhaps inviting a sibling to join it.

Competition begins very young and is at first playful. This yearling American black bear is chasing a sibling that has managed to catch a small fish.

such as marmots, whose body temperature drops from almost 97 degrees F (36 degrees C) to less than 40 degrees F (4 degrees C) accompanied by other drastic metabolic changes—only four heartbeats per minute, for example, and only one breath in about six minutes. Bears have been likened to raccoons, which den and become torpid during winter but awaken and emerge intermittently during warm spells.

But bears in northern latitudes seldom awaken—much less emerge—unless disturbed. During just the last year or two, researchers have succeeded in attaching various metabolic measuring devices to bears shortly before they denned, so that

changes could be recorded. The conclusion is that bears—at least northern bears—are true hibernators but not particularly deep hibernators. Their heartbeat does slow significantly, as does their breathing and body temperature and all their metabolic processes.

Since the mother bear is deeply asleep and the emerging cubs are exceptionally small relative to her size, their birth does not disturb her. If they were larger, she could not possibly produce sufficient milk for their sustenance and growth until they were ready for weaning—quite long after their early spring emergence from the den, although they begin to nibble solid food as soon as they can get it. The newborn cubs, more or less buried in the mother's warm fur, soon wriggle and crawl their way to her nipples (she has six) and begin nursing. While in the den they occasionally move about a little—though there isn't much room for crawling or manoeuvring—but most of their time is spent sleeping and suckling.

Growing Cubs

When they finally totter into the sunlight, they are likely to weigh 5 to 7 pounds (2.25 to 3 kilograms)—a four- or fivefold gain in weight on the nourishment of the mother's rich milk. With her cubs now scampering, tumbling, play-fighting, and exploring, she is a sometimes permissive mother, allowing them to climb all over her and even bite or tug at her. But she is also capable of delivering a corrective

With a misplaced snap or swipe, even the most experienced brown bears frequently miss passing fish. But with so many salmon swimming upstream just under the surface (and quite often partly above the surface), the bears catch all they can eat.

American black bears can swim well, but seldom do because the need to cross lakes or large rivers is infrequent, and they can walk across most of the streams in their habitat. Here a big black bear runs through the water, splashing mightily.

Polar bears are not unique in their leaping ability—and agility. Here, a young American black bear jumps a creek at a favourite crossing place.

An American black bear cub stands up to nuzzle its mother. They often stand upright to do this and when playing, and all bears occasionally rise on their hind legs while scratching their backs against tree trunks.

It is early spring, and a yearling male black bear, instinctively practising behaviour that will be of value in two or three years when it is sexually mature, scent-marks a tree. This will advertise his presence to receptive females and may reroute other males wandering the area in search of mates.

With dexterity developed from years of tireless practice, a black bear catches salmon in an Alaskan river.

or merely irritable swat, and she becomes very stern and quick about sending them up a tree or behind her at the approach of anything unfamiliar. If she is a black bear, she herself may climb trees to encourage them or just be with them.

Brown bears, having a somewhat different claw-and-paw structure as well as greater size and weight, lose their tree-climbing ability by the time they mature. A grizzly's cubs avoid danger by moving behind her and then, if feeling bold, imi-

tating her growls, head lowering (a threat gesture), and even the sudden rearing up on the hind legs—a posture that emphasises a bear's menacing size while also giving the animal an unobstructed field of vision, hearing, and smell.

Colouration

Among polar bears, those rotund little cubs will be as white as their mother, and among the tropical and subtropical species the young usually run true to the prototyp-

An Alaskan grizzly carries a salmon ashore. Grizzlies of the northwestern coast of North America grow much larger than their inland kin because their diet is enormously enriched by the spawning runs of Pacific salmon.

Whether guarding cubs or defending a kill, a bear will tolerate no intrusion and is seldom vanquished by any animal except a larger bear. Here, an American black bear confronts timber wolves and is about to rout them.

Bears sometimes raid birds' nests, but adult gulls and other birds foraging or resting near a bear can evade a lunge, so they show little fear. This brown bear may be fishing or just bathing. Bears occasionally bathe in summer to cool themselves and escape annoying insects.

Bears pursue their salmon prey with such full-scale enthusiasm that they often topple over in attempts to capture the fish.

PHOTO CREDITS